Wind in the Long Grass

A collection of Haiku

EDITED BY

WILLIAM J. HIGGINSON

ILLUSTRATED BY

Sandra Speidel

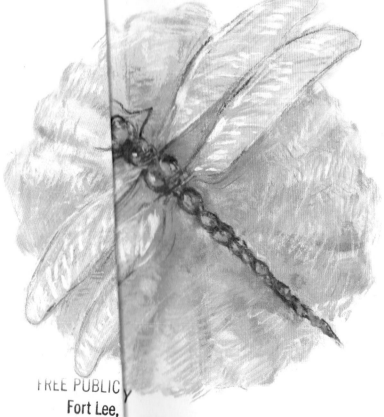

SIMON & SCHUSTER
BOOKS FOR YOUNG READERS
Published by Simon & Schuster
New York • London • Toronto • Sydney • Tokyo • Singapore

SIMON & SCHUSTER BOOKS FOR YOUNG READERS
Simon & Schuster Building, Rockefeller Center,
1230 Avenue of the Americas, New York, New York 10020.

Introduction and compilation copyright © 1991 by William J. Higgion.
Illustrations copyright © 1991 by Sandra Speidel.
All rights reserved including the right of reproduction
in whole or in part in any form.
SIMON & SCHUSTER BOOKS FOR YOUNG READERS
is a trademark of Simon & Schuster.

Designed by Vicki Kalajian
The text of this book is set in 16 pt. Usherwood Medium.
The illustrations were done in pastel.
The display type was hand-lettered by John Stevens.

Manufactured in Singapore.

10   9   8   7   6   5   4   3   2   1

Library of Congress Cataloging-in-Publication Data
Wind in the long grass : a collection of haiku /
edited by William J. Higginson : illustrated by Sandra Speidel.
Summary: An illustrated collection of haiku from all over
the world arranged by season.   1. Haiku. English—
Translations from foreign languages.   2. Haiku—Translations
into English.   3. Children's poetry, English—Translations from
foreign languages.   4. Children's poetry—Translations into English
[1. Haiku.   2. Poetry—Collections.]   I. Higginson, William J.,
II. Speidel, Sandra, ill.   PR1195.H25W56   1991   821′.0408—
89-21804   ISBN: 0-671-67978-3

This book is for William Higginson Branin,
and all children and poets and artists,
everywhere.

—W.J.H.

To my daughter Zoe, who teaches me everyday
about life's fleeting moments.

—S.S.

WHAT MAKES A HAIKU?

The haiku and pictures in this book will all make you imagine that you are seeing, hearing, smelling, tasting, or touching something in a special way.

Like all haiku, each poem here speaks of one particular event, one special time when someone sensed the world fresh and new, and found simple words to tell about it. Haiku usually show something in one season or another. Each month, even each week, day, or minute, something new happens in nature, so there is always something new to write a haiku about.

Most haiku have three lines with no rhyme—the sounds at the ends of lines do not repeat. Haiku form varies from one language to another, because no two languages have quite the same rhythms or sound patterns. And different poets, in Japan as well as around the world, write haiku their own way.

To write a haiku in English in traditional form, give your poem three lines, with two accented beats in the first line, three accented beats in the second, and two in the third. You don't have to do it the same way every time, though.

Write about things people can see, hear, taste, touch, or smell—or some combination. If you see the way a thing looks, hear the way it sounds, and can put words together so that other people see and hear the same thing in their minds, you can write haiku. Enjoy!

William J. Higginson

SPRING

how does that glow
on the clouds come
without trombones

M. M. Nichols
USA

wind:
the long hairs
on my neck

Larry Wiggin
USA

a pair of pigeons
in a mist of spring rain
shoulder to shoulder

Anton Gerits
NETHERLANDS

On the smooth plow handle
the calloused hand
of the old farmer

John J. Carey
CANADA

sitting
sand in hand
the sand
is warm

Seisensui Ogiwara
JAPAN

one by one
he hands over the spring winds:
the balloon seller

Kazuo Satō
JAPAN

bird singing
in the dark: I try
to get out of my dream

Virginia Brady Young
USA

On the branch of a tree
a bird
weighs itself.

Pablo Mora
MEXICO

on the snowy road
the feet of the sparrows
seem to hop again

Patrick Blanche
FRANCE

misty trees—
the distant gleaming
became a heron

Shūson Katō
JAPAN

Holding the water,
held by it—
the dark mud.

William J. Higginson
USA

Flood of lilacs,
she brings flowers in her hands
and in her eyes.

Rafael Lozano
MEXICO

sunset
in the jar on the windowsill
dandelions close

Karen Sohne
USA

SUMMER

distant thunder
the dog's toenails click
against the linoleum

Gary Hotham
USA

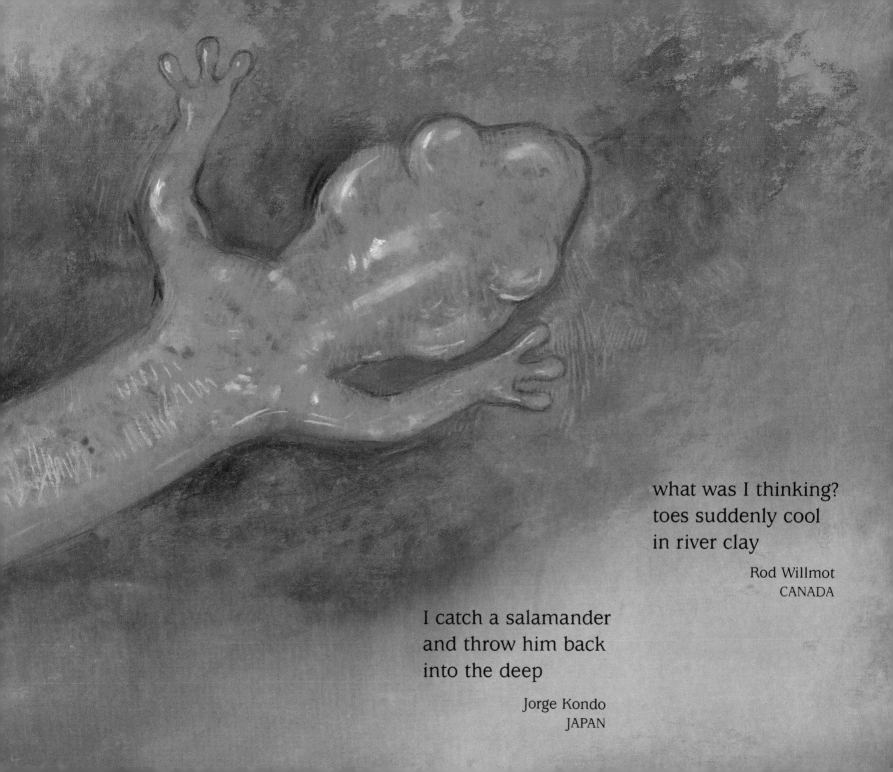

what was I thinking?
toes suddenly cool
in river clay

Rod Willmot
CANADA

I catch a salamander
and throw him back
into the deep

Jorge Kondo
JAPAN

Across the meadow
the slow moving tongues
of grazing cows.

Piet Zandboer
NETHERLANDS

the cat on the roof-edge
measures the space
licks its paws

Jean Antonini
FRANCE

hailstorm cleared up—
now all stretched out
the hills and rivers

Kijō Murakami
JAPAN

the potato thieves
exclaim in low voices
at the falling star

Dee Evetts
ENGLAND

wind in the long grass
and somebody
whistling...

Marianne Bluger
CANADA

this clear morning
a couple of rose petals
in the spider web

Elizabeth Searle Lamb
USA

sunglasses on—
the color
of the deserted sea

Yoshiko Inoue
JAPAN

Sea:
The night has dappled you
with white and black.

Carlos Suárez Veintimilla
ECUADOR

at the sea's edge
grandpa skips a few stones
before they go

Allan Curry
CANADA

AUTUMN

the moonlit evening
gathers waves of
young maidens' teeth

Kinichi Sawaki
JAPAN

Traversing the web
the clear shining moon
keeps the spider awake.

José Juan Tablada
MEXICO

Under the moon
just the little willow leaves
shedding their own light.

Aleksandar Nejgebauer
YUGOSLAVIA

the mountain darkens
I listen to the voice of the mountain

Santōka Taneda
JAPAN

walking out into
more and more
stars

Carl Patrick
USA

again covering
the sleeping children the sounds
of night waves

Hakusen Kubo
JAPAN

The hurricane left me
no roof. Swallow, where
shall we go off to?

Eduardo Benet y Castellón
CUBA

fog…
just the tree and I
at the bus stop

Jerry Kilbride
USA

chill west wind—
my shawl smells
of camphor

Melodee Unthank
AUSTRALIA

Labour Day
back home from the cottage
June on the calendar

Jocelyne Villeneuve
CANADA

dragonfly
on my fingernail
looks at me

Penny Harter
USA

from the attic window
finally touched
the empty dove's nest

Selma Stefanile
USA

WINTER

the smell of the iron
as I come down the stairs
winter evening

Lee Gurga
USA

on the road
starlight—gives me
an icicle

Shugyō Takaha
JAPAN

Puff, Puff, Puff
the first white flakes fall
and soon winter.

Teresio Raineri
ITALY

snowed in
the gardener telling secrets
long distance

LeRoy Gorman
CANADA

snowfall
Christmas lights on the birdhouse

Cor van den Heuvel
USA

She cut out the dark
figure of a timber wolf
with scarlet scissors

Michael Bradford Stillman
USA

a hawk circling—
the ruins of the Incas
just stones

Yōichi Iwata
BRAZIL

passing whale's eye…
the islands on the horizon
sink and rise again

Larry Gates
USA

winter morning
without leaf or flower
the shape of the tree

L. A. Davidson
USA

let the clouds come too!
let the people play in the forest
of winter trees!

Ippekirō Nakatsuka
JAPAN

cemetery…
leaves chasing
Cadillacs

Jack Stamm
JAPAN

The great stream is silent
only sometimes it sounds quietly
deep under the ice.

Imma von Bodmershof
GERMANY

The abandoned canoe
on the blue waters
pitches peacefully toward the horizon.

Mboye Gueye
SENEGAL

BEYOND THE SEASONS

River at twilight:
I watch the darkness flow
into my eyes

George Swede
CANADA

In the Museum Garden

Empty chairs
the statues returned
to the other museum.

George Seferis
GREECE

the heated argument done
I go to the street
and become a motorcycle

Tohta Kaneko
JAPAN

Voices
of transparent beings
in the child's room.

Carlos Alabes
COLOMBIA

Streetcar rumble
kept me awake last night
puts me to sleep

Chris Faiers
CANADA

ACKNOWLEDGEMENTS

The editor thanks Pamela Pollack, who pushed this book through to completion; Sylvia Frezzolini and the art department, who made it a labor of love; Sandra Speidel, who made it glow; Bonnie R. Crown, who never lost faith in it; Sharon Weathers, who asked for it; Penny Harter, who helped it through three lives; and the following good persons, who helped greatly with locating and translating the poems: Manya Bean, Anthony A. Brazina, Jean C. Carlson, André Duhaime, Mireille von Ehrenfels-Abeille, Petra Engelbert, Dee Evetts, Constanze Ferenčik, Sherrie Gianpolo-Woody, Jeff Goldschmidt, Ty Hadman, Penny Harter, Dorothy Howard, Marie Iaconangelo, R. E. T. Johnson, Kozue Kobayashi, Tadashi Kondo, Elizabeth Searle Lamb, Peter Liao, Donald Montauti, Wanda Reumer, Kazuo Satō, Jack Stamm, Maria Sutcliffe, Sonō Uchida, Cor van den Heuvel, Nina Zivancevic. Unless otherwise indicated in the copyright notices below, all translations are by William J. Higginson.

Every effort has been made to contact copyright holders. The editor would be pleased to hear from any copyright holders not acknowledged below.

In the following listing HH refers to *The Haiku Handbook: How to Write, Share, and Teach Haiku* by William J. Higginson with Penny Harter, published by Kodansha International; *IHC* refers to *International Haiku Contest Work Collection* published by The Modern Haiku Association of Japan.

"Voices" by Carlos Alabes, copyright © 1988 Carlos Alabes, from *Kanora* edited by Humberto Senegal, by permission of Humberto Senegal.

"the cat on the roof-edge" by Jean Antonini, copyright © 1987 Jean Antonini, from *IHC*, by permission of the author.

"The hurricane left me" by Eduardo Benet y Castellón, copyright © 1957 Eduardo Benet y Castellón, from *Ensayo de Haikai Antillano* published by Excelsior; translation by R. E. T. Johnson from "The Cuban Issa", *Modern Haiku* 5:4, 41; copyright © 1974 Kay Titus Mormino, by permission of Robert Spiess.

"On the snowy road" by Patrick Blanche, copyright © 1987 Patrick Blanche, from *IHC*, by permission of the author.

"The great stream is silent" by Imma von Bodmershof, copyright © Albert Langen Georg Müller Verlag 1962, from *Haiku* published by Albert Langen Georg Müller, by permission of Mireille von Ehrenfels-Abeille; translation by William J. Higginson, from *HH*, copyright © 1985 William J. Higginson; by permission of the translator.

"wind in the long grass" by Marianne Bluger, © Les éditions Asticou enrg. 1985, from *Haiku: anthologie canadienne* edited by Dorothy Howard and André Duhaime, published by Les éditions Asticou enrg.; by permission of the author.

"On the smooth plow handle" by John J. Carey, © 1988 John J. Carey, from *Tidepool*; by permission of the author.

"at the sea's edge" by Allan Curry, copyright © 1989 Allan Curry, by permission of the author.

"winter morning" by L. A. Davidson, copyright © 1982 L. A. Davidson, from *The Shape of the Tree* published by Wind Chimes; by permission of the author.

"the potato thieves" by Dee Evetts, copyright © 1988 Dee Evetts, from *A Small Ceremony* published by From Here Press; by permission of the author.

"Streetcar rumble" by Chris Faiers, © Les éditions Asticou enrg. 1985, from *Haiku: anthologie canadienne* edited by Dorothy Howard and André Duhaime, published by Les éditions Asticou enrg.; by permission of the author.

"passing whale's eye . . ." by Larry Gates, copyright © 1988 Larry Gates, from *An Anthology of Haiku by People of the United States and Canada* published by Japan Air Lines; by permission of the author.

"a pair of pigeons" by Anton Gerits, copyright 1984 Anton Gerits, from *Alleen wanneer ik kijk* published by De Oude Degel, by permission of the author; translation by William J. Higginson, from *HH*, copyright © 1985 William J. Higginson, by permission of the translator.

"snowed in" by LeRoy Gorman, copyright © 1987 LeRoy Gorman, by permission of the author.

"The abandoned canoe" by Mboye Gueye, © Éditions Techniques Nord-Africaines 1983, from *Haiku: le poème le plus court du monde* by Sonō Uchida, published by Editions Techniques Nord-Africaines; by permission of Sonō Uchida.

"the smell of the iron" by Lee Gurga, copyright © 1988 Lee Gurga, from *A mouse pours out* published by High / Coo Press; by permission of the author.

"dragonfly" by Penny Harter, copyright © 1987 Penny Harter, from *IHC*, by permission of the author.

"Holding the water," by William J. Higginson, copyright © 1987 William J. Higginson, from *Ten Years' Collected Haiku*, Vol. 1, published by From Here Press; by permission of the author.

"distant thunder" by Gary Hotham, © 1979 Gary Hotham, from *Against the Linoleum* published by Yiqralo Press; by permission of the author.

"sunglasses on—" by Yoshiko Inoue, © Kōdansha 1981, from *Gendai Joryū Haiku Zenshū* published by Kōdansha; by permission of Kōdansha.

"a hawk circling—" by Yōichi Iwata, copyright © 1987 Yōichi Iwata, from *IHC*, by permission of the author.

"the heated argument done" by Tohta Kaneko, copyright © 1961 Tohta Kaneko, from *Kaneko Tohta Kushū* published by Asahi Shinbun Sha; by permission of the author.

"misty trees—" by Shūson Katō, copyright © 1977 Shūson Katō, from *Saishin haiku saijiki* edited by Kenkichi Yamamoto, published by Bungei shunjū; by permission of the author.

"fog . . ." by Jerry Kilbride, copyright © Japan Air Lines 1988, from *Newsweek Japan*, by permission of the author.

"I catch a salamander" by Jorge Kondo, copyright © 1989 Jorge Kondo, by permission of the author.

"again covering" by Hakusen Kubo, copyright © 1919 Hakusen Kubo, from *Sōun*; by permission of Mitsu Tamura.

"this clear morning" by Elizabeth Searle Lamb, copyright © 1987 Elizabeth Searle Lamb, from *IHC*, by permission of the author.

"Flood of lilacs," by Rafael Lozano, © Ty Hadman 1987, from *Breve historia y antologia del haikú en la lirica mexicana* by Ty Hadman, published by Editorial Domés, S.A.; by permission of the publisher.

"On the branch of a tree" by Pablo Mora, © Ty Hadman 1987, from *Breve Historia y antologia del haikú en la lirica mexicana* by Ty Hadman, published by Editorial Domés, S.A.; by permission of the publisher.

"let the clouds come too!" by Ippekirō Nakatsuka, copyright © 1938 Ippekirō Nakatsuka, from *Wakaba-yashi*; by permission of Mayumi Nakatsuka.

"Under the moon" by Aleksandar Nejgebauer, copyright © 1977 Aleksandar Nejgebauer, from *Haiku*; translation by William J. Higginson, from *HH*, copyright © 1985 William J. Higginson; by permission of the translator.

"how does that glow" by M. M. Nichols, copyright © 1989 M. M. Nichols, by permission of the author.

"walking out into" by Carl Patrick, copyright © 1989 Carl Patrick, by permission of the author.

"sitting" by Seisensui Ogiwara, copyright © 1964 Seisensui Ogiwara, from *A History of Haiku* by R. H. Blyth; translation by Hokuseido, by permission of Kaiichi Ogihara.

"Puff, Puff, Puff" by Teresio Raineri, copyright © 1987 Teresio Raineri, from *IHC*, by permission of the author.

"one by one" by Kazuo Satō, copyright © 1987 Kazuo Satō, by permission of the author.

"starlit night" by Kinichi Sawaki, copyright © 1977 Kinichi Sawaki, from *Gendai Haiku Jiten*, published by Kadokawa Shoten; by permission of the author.

"In the Museum Garden" by George Seferis, copyright © Icaros 1940, from *Tetradio Gymnasmaton* published by Icaros; translation by Manya Bean, copyright © 1985 Manya Bean and William J. Higginson, from *HH*, by permission of the translator.

"sunset" by Karen Sohne, © 1988 Karen Sohne, from *the sound of the stream* published by Wind Chimes; by permission of the author.

"from the attic window" by Selma Stefanile, copyright © 1977 Selma Stefanile, from *Sparrow 33: Minnow*; by permission of the author.

"cemetery . . ." by Jack Stamm, copyright © 1989 Jack Stamm, by permission of the author.

"She cut out the dark" by Michael Bradford Stillman, copyright © 1976 Michael Bradford Stillman, from *An Eye of Minnows* published by Indigo; by permission of the author.

"River at twilight:" by George Swede, © 1983 George Swede, from *Tick Bird: Poems for Children* published by Three Trees Press; by permission of the author.

"Traversing the web" by José Juan Tablada, copyright © Universidad Nacional Autónoma de México 1971, from *Obras, I — Poesia* published by Univ. National Autónoma de México; by permission of the publisher.

"on the road" by Shugyō Takaha, copyright © 1977 Shugyō Takaha, from *Gendai Haiku Jiten* published by Kadokawa Shoten; by permission of Shugyō Takaha.

"chill west wind—" by Melodee Unthank, copyright © 1979 Melodee Unthank.

"snowfall" by Cor van den Heuvel, copyright © 1988 Cor van den Heuvel, by permission of the author.

"Labour Day" by Jocelyne Villeneuve, copyright © 1988 Jocelyne Villeneuve, from *Special Delivery* published by Haiku Canada; by permission of the author.

"wind." by Larry Wiggin, copyright © Cor van den Heuvel 1986, from *The Haiku Anthology* published by Simon & Schuster; by permission of Ruth Wiggins.

"Sea:" by Carlos Suárez Veintimilla, copyright © 1951, from *Abside*.

"what was I thinking?" by Rod Willmot, copyright © 1984 Rod Willmot, from *The Ribs of Dragonfly* published by Black Moss Press; by permission of the author.

"bird singing" by Virginia Brady Young, copyright © 1982 Virginia Brady Young, from *Waterfall* published by Timberline Press; by permission of the author.

"Across the meadow" by Piet Zandboer, from *Samen Oud Worden*, by permission of the author; translation by William J. Higginson, from *HH*, copyright © 1985 William J. Higginson; by permission of the translator.